LOST
IN THE
GREENWOOD

LOST IN THE GREENWOOD

Poems

ELLEN ROBERTS YOUNG

atmosphere press

For Susan Bagby, who gave me the bookmark,
and Sandra Kohler, my writing partner,
who both encouraged me throughout the project.

CONTENTS

I. Enchantment

HOW IT BEGAN

A gift from a friend,
museum bookmark: a lady
with loose yellow hair tightly woven.
I am entangled.

She's a figure from a wall hanging,
one of a series with unicorns,
lions and banners,
six ladies finely clothed,
flowers, monkeys, rabbits
and trees: oak, holly,
orange, pine. Stretched

like wool being spun into thread,
I am dragged into a world
of artists, weavers, dyers,
mystery and magnificence,
by a loose strand of hair
tightly woven.

1. Enchantment

ENCHANTMENT

Can you be lost in the woods
in a valley of fields
where the trees are set out
in rows straight as streets
that cross at right angles
and your mother rarely
holds up a mirror?

No unicorns came to drink
in the creek I played beside.

The glass on the wall
held no magic power.

Tiger lilies and tiger
swallowtails were
enchantment enough.
Unicorns stayed away
until I grew hungry for
darker mysteries, the pull
of their wild power.

STASIS

("The Unicorn is Attacked" from the Met Unicorn
Tapestries)

> [N]o stag, in a situation like this, could escape
> the hunters' spears; only a unicorn could do
> that.
>> Freeman, *The Unicorn Tapestries* (1976)

The designer places the prey
in a stag-like pose. Three scenting hounds
track the beast in water. Spears
at angles point to their moment of triumph.
Greyhounds, by their masters, watch.
Not one of the dutiful dogs
opens his mouth to bay.

Below, violet flowers give way
to daisies, pomegranates swell, partridges
court in the not-yet of May. Above,
two hornmen blow. Do they not know?
The unicorn cannot yet be caught.

PULLED IN

My eyes, drawn first to the large white
patch that is the unicorn, see more
on each revisit.

Has one of the rabbits moved?
Has the hyena drooled?
The lion is undisturbed.

It cannot be that these thick leaves
don't rustle as my glance sways
toward them and away.

The crush of creatures presses me
to ponder how converging lines
of perspective narrow my world.

Linear time's string of tomorrows
allows no return. The unicorn cannot
live again in this straitened age.

OLDEN DAYS

In a world of kings, lords, ladies,
servants, serfs, tradesmen, artists,
        maidens, fair by definition, were
        by elegant dress made beautiful.

In those days, mirrors gleamed, newly
made of fine glass, mesmerizing.
        Human coupling and the greening
        of the land could not be disentwined.

When dyers turned crushed plants
into red, yellow and blue thread,
        weavers came to buy the thread
        as patrons ordered their weavings.

In those days, narwhal tusks, harvested far
to the north, were sold as unicorn horns.
        Unicorns lived
        in tapestries hung on walls.

COLORS

Red made from roots of madder,
yellow from everything but the roots
of weld, the challenge is blue:
woad leaves dried, fermented, spread
on stone for nine stinky weeks.

From India Vasco da Gama
brings indigo, a better blue.

Before science can prove
the chemical's the same, central heat
warms walls; tapestries are not needed.

Fiber artists experiment
with knots, loops, uneven strings
of burgundy or aquamarine, loose

as lines of free verse
hanging from a margin.

Red and blue give way to cyan,
magenta; synthesized hues
to dye threads or print reproductions.
Machine-woven carpets of many colors
comfort my bare feet.

HUNTING THE UNICORN

Hounds at the ready, young men lifting spears
follow the prince to whom their fealty's sworn
into the greenwood where the beast appears.

Gathering at the edge where forest clears
they'll hunt the bold, elusive unicorn,
hounds at the ready, young men lifting spears.

Noblemen with servants and their peers
pursue him for the healing in his horn
deep in the greenwood where the beast appears.

Far into the chase, the creature reappears
held by a virgin saintly and well-born,
while hounds stand ready, young men lift their spears.

Hounds now at heel, trumpet blasts in their ears,
men come to the castle, their quarry borne
out of the greenwood where the beast appears.

Lady, lord, and hunters shed no tears,
believing their prey is, phoenix-like, reborn.
Alas for ready hounds, young men with spears.
Though green the wood, the beast no more appears.

INITIATION

("The Hunters Enter the Woods" from the Met
Unicorn Tapestries)

Most fair, sweet son—exquisite, tender flesh—
Romance of the Rose, line 12999

Observe this handsome youth in central place.
With a curious eye he looks around,
letting the plumed hat of his rank slip down.
Of three companions, he's the freshest face.
No weariness disturbs his natural grace;
he seems innocent as the floral ground
enclosing the scene, while handlers and hounds
are on alert, ready to join the chase.

Ahead of him, no mere run in the wood,
no play at swords. Struggle and sacrifice
will mar his skin, while the need of heirs, choice
of a good marriage, readily poured blood
in hunt and combat, will teach him command
of self, and turn this eager boy to man.

THE DONOR OF THE HUNT OF THE UNICORN TAPESTRIES PROPOSES A TOAST

Friends, I propose, as elder at this board,
a toast to lineage and to our Lords,
honoring first our gracious Lord in heaven,
next, good King Louis, His regent. Now, then,
come toast with me the pair whose marriage knot
is oft repeated in this fiber art,
my gift. To celebrate this alliance
I conceived a set of weavings with dense
growing woods, no fussy mille fleurs background
but living trees and flowers that flourish round
our own properties. Once we were banned
from hunting even on our private land;
I was a boy when Charles renewed that right
in '84 and I am certain we would fight
not to lose it again. Precious to me
the green woods featured in these tapestries.

Before I'd fully settled on the theme
I hired an artist to lay out the scheme,
charged him to include a wide selection
of the verdure coming under your protection.
What within? No saints or heroes nor horns
calling to war would do. I thought of unicorns.
The artist I employed was first dismayed,
he pondered how the beast should be portrayed,
then leapt to it. He let the stag-like form
decide his plan, though horses are the norm
in stag hunts. Men with sword and spear
and hounds – admire these graceful hounds! so dear
to me and all who love the hunt, its scents
of closing chase, its heart-stirring moments.

But for the unicorn a maiden must
be there to tame, to conquer. Is this just
an interruption? No, it amplifies.
As many meanings touch our daily lives,
here let them be combined to see and show
the things of heaven and the things below.
I'd have preferred her lap should hold his head,
like Christ with Mary. No, the artist said,
the mirror's de rigueur. In any case
the gentle balances the bold. Please place
these in your bedroom. All the wealth
of plants will bring fertility and health.
This merger of our houses, may it thrive,
bring many sons to keep our line alive,
a daughter who may wed . . . . Join me, drinking
a toast to this couple and to our king,
and to the other Lord you're sworn to serve;
I pray His mercy may us all preserve.

SERVANTS OF THE SUN

Why hunt the unicorn? No common prey
is he, no stag or boar to head a feast.
Men are creatures of boisterous day,

the sun, while like the quiet moon this beast
is gentle and a healer of the streams
from poison. Protector of the least,

he should be revered, respected. Yet dreams
of slaughter rise, enflamed men burn
to conquer him, an enemy he seems.

Blessing spirit he is; do spirits turn?
Perceiving this one as threat, they go
in pursuit. Unable, unwilling to learn

they cannot control the hidden flow
of imagination, they seek to bring
him down with hefty spears, wishing no

restriction on their rule. How can they sing
praises to Christ while they strive to remove
this symbol of incarnation? See, they ring

him with hounds, thinking they can improve
the world by driving mystery out
of the woods. It's hubris, that move.

A deep desire for the light makes them doubt,
distrust the shifting moon, for they are sworn
as servants of the sun. No one can flout

the balance of opposites. We can only mourn
the way a streak of violence seasons
each man's virtue. Spirit, moon, unicorn:
Why hunt the creature? Men have their reasons.

ALL THE PIECES PUT IN PLACE

("The Unicorn is Found" from the Met Unicorn
Tapestries)

> "... the essential features of the late medieval
> mind [include] the inclination to regard every
> detail as an independent entity ...
> Johan Huizinga, *The Autumn of the
> Middle Ages* (1923)

The situation: a poisoned stream.

Lion, lioness, panther, genet face
    a hungry hyena, good against evil.

A stag, larger than the lion
    has scared away the snake.

Birds in pairs, rabbits run off to mate.

The men are twelve, chatting, ignorant
    as Christ's disciples at supper.

Strawberry, daisy, pansy say spring;
    roses say Mary.

A pheasant sees his reflection, portent
    of the unicorn's fate.

Unicorn's horn touches, purifies the water.

Water of life from the fountain of Eden.

The spotter points to the prey;
    the chase begins.

LOST IN THE GREENWOOD

These tapestries encourage close attention
and every second glance raises a question.

Who is the youth, who is the boy with a dog,
why is the servant bringing food and grog?

In lively action can we pull apart
what was reality from what is art?

Do violets speak of love or of the dead—
and who is the side-glancing lady in red?

I read, I study, each puzzle explained
raises new issues. What then have I gained?

Why so much oak and holly—What are the odds
they are meant to represent pre-Christian gods?

How much can one generation edit
the rich tradition that is handed to it?

With unicorns is everything pretense?
He's killed and yet alert inside a fence.

Who designed, who made these? What's unknown
extends in every path beyond the known.
Dare I make up theories of my own?

STREAM IN THE FOREST

Weavings depict a forest, holly and oak,
and a hunt to celebrate a marriage.
Men equipped with spear, sword and horn
trample on daffodils and violets
in eternal spring. A pomegranate
flourishes beside a flowing stream.

Water out of a fountain feeds the stream
flowing from panel to panel, oak,
hawthorn, rooted nearby. A pomegranate
tops the fountain, promises marriage
fertile as its many seeds, while violets
wave to the air of many a blowing horn.

Do they hunt the unicorn for his horn,
these well-armed men? Their prey leaps the stream
like a stag, gores a dog. Violets
will drip with blood, yet spears, tough as oak,
are useless. Nature's signs blend marriage
and faith, Christ's blood and the pomegranate.

Red juice falls from a burst pomegranate.
The maiden has touched the unicorn's horn.
She is ready, accepting the marriage
as Mary accepted a birth. Now the stream
can nourish cherry, ash, orange and oak,
carnations, roses, campion, violets.

All seasons at once: iris and violets
beside ripe fruits. Persephone's pomegranate
foretells Demeter's planting when the oak
flowers. In cycles of harvest a horn
of plenty from all these trees will stream,
for the country is blessed by this marriage.

The hunt affirms that an offer of marriage
is more than giving bouquets of violets
and sitting together beside a stream.
There is blood, red as the pomegranate,
sexual power in the unicorn's horn.
Ancient connections encircle the oak:

marriage and death in the pomegranate,
promise of violets, healing in a horn,
a life-giving stream for humans as for oak.

PERSPECTIVES

> We must remember that we are all,
> like it or not, hothouse products.
>> Lucien Febvre,
>> *Life in Renaissance France* (1925)

         No distance.
Sky and castle a near backdrop; trees,
unicorn, dogs, hunters, holly
squeeze
toward the front plane.
A shouldered spear could pierce
a companion's neck, a blowing horn blast
the neighbor's eardrum. (The tale
is told by accretion of detail.)

         No breeze
carries scent of fruit or stirs leaves
of this scene dense with details,
airless
as a smoky kitchen where
owners, servants, hired hands eat
together, stifling as innovation is stifled
by weavers' guilds. (Business is good,
it should be fairly shared.)

         Unbound
by tradition, painters play with mirrors,
teach their patrons to read their
strokes
as distance, designs in paint
as views of a world extending

beyond the plane. Weavers do not
pursue this new idea. (Their
business is booming.)

                               Windows
grown large and common, painting returns
to surface, brush marks on canvas,
wall.
Would our heated houses, noise
of machines, chemical odors, feel airless,
narrow, to those who filled old kitchens?
(They could, more easily than we,
enjoy the stars.)

UNDER THE APPLE TREE

(Fragments of Lost Panel from the Met Unicorn
Tapestries)

> Father Latomia, ... of the Society of Jesus, to
> counteract infidelity and immorality among
> the students, made a vow at the end of the
> eighteenth century to devote the month of
> May to Mary.
> Frederick Holweck,
> *Catholic Encyclopedia* (1912)

It is August, season of harvest
and the turn toward dark.
Apples are ripe. The woman
whose hand holds the unicorn
is virgin, is Mary, is pagan
goddess of love and death.
Believers who argue over rites
and forms accept this blend.

May is made Mary's month,
apple trees in bloom, devotions
prescribed to counteract its
dangers: the heavy-scented
hawthorn, secret trysts, youth's
energy cascading. Attach
blue ribbons to Mary's shrine,
forget the maypole's colors.

August slows the rhythm.
When all of Italy goes on vacation
Mary's assumption, made dogma,
removes her from the unicorn,
lifts her whole to heaven, away
from harvest's dirt and death,
separate from gutsy goddesses,
pure as the distant moon.

THE LADY OF THE HOUSE CONSIDERS
HER DUTIES

> This lady will gladly read instructive books
> about good manners and behavior and
> sometimes devotion.
> > Christine de Pizan, *The Treasure*
> > *of the City of Ladies* (c. 1405)

Devotion, in Miss Christine's eyes,
can easily be overdone.
She wants her ladies worldly wise,
her caution list goes on and on.

Beware loose tongues, she says, deceit
that flatters, and avoid excess
in all, be kind, but be discreet.
She sees a never-ending press,

as if the dogs that hunt the white
beast I see on our tapestry
were at my heels all day, all night,
threatening ill. I don't agree.

I'm busy tending his affairs
at home when my Lord goes to war,
but don't neglect my daily prayers
for safe return. I build our store

of credit with the deity.
Knowing my role, a thread not placed
too high or low, I've certainty
my prayers help keep us firmly based,

our home, society and land
woven together, tight, secure.
Preserved and guided by the hand
of God this world will long endure.

CHECKMATE

> Mr. Rorimer also believed that the lord and lady
> of the castle, receiving the procession of hunters
> bringing the dead unicorn, could be identified
> as Queen Anne and her husband, King Louis XII.
> Freeman, *The Unicorn Tapestries* (1976)

Anne, ruler of Brittany at eleven
     for her Duchy's protection marries
         young Charles, king of France.

Their infant son dies, the crown
     passes to cousin Louis,
         who wants Anne for his own.

As Queen, the Duchess of Brittany must
     provide her king a son. Not prayer
         nor pilgrimage nor unicorns suffice.

Though Anne bears several children, only
     two daughters live. One will succeed
         her mother as duchess.

Could it be Louis and Anne receiving the dead
     unicorn on the tapestry? Then the boy
         behind them, whose son is he?

Louis, having no son, commits Anne's daughter
     to the cousin next in line. Brittany
         must be wife of France again.

OFFERING

("The Unicorn is Killed and Brought to the Castle"
from the Met Unicorn Tapestries)

> ... it would seem highly probable that the
> castle depicted in this panel is meant to
> represent Hades, and that the lord and lady are
> the king and queen of the infernal region.
> John Williamson, *The Oak King,*
> *the Holly King and the Unicorn* (1986)

A crowd has gathered at the gate, watchers
by twos and threes peer from walls, windows.
A procession brings the dead beast out of the woods
whole, no customary division among hunters
and hounds. In the upper left the kill,
as if in a speech balloon, the story
as the hunters tell it, incomplete,
the slaying of a stag.

Is this Hades? Then the honored figures
are Pluto and Persephone, receiving Christ
who's come to rake over hell, rescue the innocents.
Or is this King Louis, known by his nose,
and his Queen Anne? The artist
tells two stories at once, as he has
from the start, faith and life
entwined, indivisible.

Who is the boy, tenderly holding his dog?
He is the artist's prayer for the king's
succession, an heir the gift of the unicorn,
the unicorn, gift of his subjects.

AT THE RIGHT TIME

> The cycle of the seasons was a vital reflection
> of human life to the people of the Middle Ages.
> John Williamson, *The Oak King,*
> *the Holly King and the Unicorn* (1986)

A unicorn cannot be pursued,
caught, in a day as a stag might.

His flight carries him from Easter
to May Day to midsummer.

Spirit of fertility—first fields,
then fruit of trees, the crying newborn—

he runs on to mid-August, to Michaelmas,
a chase through all the green seasons.

The water of life flows through them all.
At harvest he may be taken.

CAUGHT

He's a hefty beast, but I cannot
ride him, cannot rest my head
against his broad shoulder,

or comb his beard. He's my
unreachable moon, my
white whale. How equip

a ship to cross this distance?
Spears strike at him like harpoons;
he does not die.

Whether he stands at attention
or runs from hounds,
he is not spooked by my presence.

My heart adjusts its rhythm
to the beating of his hooves.

11. Seeing

SEEING

I begin with one female figure, notice
how weaving portrays loose hair and brocade,
widen my view to tent, heraldic animals,
standards with arms, five more panels,
different yet similar, each on an oval of ground,
surrounded by flowers and small animals.

My search for "unicorn tapestries" brings up
another set, seven scenes, the unicorn
hunted in thick green woods. I turn
from one to the other.

A rose series   a green series

woman's world   man's world

    only the unicorn in common

here he's a servant   here a hunted beast.

Jean Le Viste ordered
the rose panels—for what occasion,
for which of his three daughters?
Lion and unicorn hold up
his standards.

           The hunt celebrates a wedding,
           of A and E, whoever they were,
           with a knotted cord. The lion
           here is quiet, neither partner
           nor threat to the unicorn.

Trees rise at the sides
like attendants, oak, pine
holly, orange, in bloom
and fruit at once.

> Oak, holly, birch, ash,
> cherry, pomegranate. A crowd
> of hunters in a crowd of trees,
> flowers of all seasons,
> hounds in ornate collars,
> men in square-toed shoes.

This woman's dog suggests
fidelity in marriage. That girl
has neither dog nor servant.
One woman is seated,
holds a mirror. The unicorn
is caught by his reflection.

> In the green wood too, despite
> hounds and spears, the unicorn
> is subdued by a woman. His head
> is not in her lap, his eye is bright.
> He is trapped by a mirror.

> His capture is what both series' makers know
> about a unicorn. The clear glass mirror
> is new in their century.

THE SPEECH OF FLOWERS

("Smell" panel from the Lady and Unicorn tapestries)

She winds carnations with a gentle hand
into the cording of a sturdy band.
In alternating color, she connects
the finest specimens. What she rejects
her monkey sniffs and grabs like contraband.

With blossoms transient yet all so grand,
twist by twist making a chaplet planned
to please the absent lover she expects,
                    she winds carnations.

Sign of betrothal, of commitment, and
a token of the rich gifts of the land,
the favored lady carefully selects
another bloom and step by step perfects
her offering, as with a gentle hand
                    she winds carnations.

ACCOMPLISHMENTS MAKE THE LADY

("Hearing" panel from the Lady and Unicorn
tapestries)

A servant pushes bellows,
her mistress touches keys
of a polished table organ.

How long must she practice
to be called accomplished?

Lion and unicorn
carry sculpted poles,
bodies facing outward.

Their heads, ears, lean in
toward the woman musing.

The bored maid could stop
the sounding if she would;
her mind is far away.

Below a hound stares at
a young wolf. All are in pause,

except six scattered rabbits,
twelve ears on the alert,
expecting sound in the silence.

COMPANION

Meeting you, Lady, in these six
panels, I rediscover a friend:
the figure who walked into
a girl/woman's wish-dreams,
my own invention, I thought.
I wished to stand out so I set you
high on a castle wall. Wishing
to dance, I dressed you in chiffon.

On the stage of my imagination
you could do anything. I, seized
by a cold, sniffling in my chair,
wishing for energy, put you at risk,
seized by dangerous men, rescued,
not a Helen or a Cassandra,
carried off like a suitcase,
you would come back safe.

Girl of my dreams, I name you
Rose, blossom, transient treasure,
companion of half-forgotten days.
Come down from that cold parapet;
that was not your place, nor mine.
I leave you to your bower, your
brocade, your jewels, your power
of self while I reclaim my own.

TASTEFUL

("Taste" panel from the Lady and Unicorn tapestries)

A woman young, bejeweled, richly dressed
with dainty fingers feeds her parakeet.
An eager monkey gobbles near her feet.
She's taught the handsome bird to keep its seat
on her gloved fist; as she picks a fruit, juicy, red
this lady who discloses no desire.

Beside a pole bearing her father's crest
the lady's servant lowers a dish to meet
her lady's hand. While bird and monkey eat,
a dog's uplifted face seems to plead
where's mine? She's trained him not to beg,
his mistress who discloses no desire.

Though blessed, in truth, she's tightly pressed.
Her father's love and longing to defeat
death has driven her to this retreat
among his banners, set up to entreat
future visitors to show him honor, led
by his daughter, who discloses no desire.

Is self-control maintained by hidden fire?
So elegant, so proper, so discreet,
this lady who discloses no desire.

HER WORLD AND HIS

(The rose tapestries and the green)

> Now none is more sagacious than the Dog,
> for he has more perception than other animals
> and he alone recognizes his own name.
> *Cambridge Bestiary* (13th Century)

He and she,
different as red and green,

both love dogs, his scenting hounds
and greyhounds, her patient, long-haired pup.

Does he bring his dogs, fresh from a muddy run
into the house? Does her pet growl or cower?

In the lady's bower, mud is unwelcome,
even on her beloved's boots.

She does not follow the chattering maids
out the gate to greet the hunters. She can wait.

He will enter her walled garden washed
clean and combed as her pet, a gentled man.

JEAN'S LAMENT

(Jean Le Viste, original owner of the Lady and Unicorn
tapestries)

The honor I desired the most was not
bestowed: I did so long to be d'Arcy
not plain Le Viste. With skill in law I left
Lyon, pursuing Louis's dream: a state
too strong to be brought down by warring kin.
This seemed a chance to join the noble class
for service to the king. My sovereign died.
Young Charles respects me as his father's man,
advisor, councilor, but he can see
nobility in feats of war alone.
He's gone to Italy to lead his troops.
Finance to him is all for raising armies.
I offer justice in the Court of Aides,
intent to guard the royal coffers. This
essential service has its good rewards;
I've gained much benefit—but title, none.
So be it. At least I've married well;
my children would be nobles if a mother's
birth were marked. A son might reach the height
that I did not. I have three daughters.
So be it. God commands us each to do
our best with what we have. My Genevieve
suggested quiet tapestries to guide
our girls in virtue and in duty too,
restraint that she's imparted by example,
as well as discipline. May they advance
to her accomplishments with grace and poise.
We shelter them against temptation lest

the new technologies of print and glass
turn them vain or lead their minds to wander
into unseemly paths of sentiment.
A daughter may give birth to noble son.
Though still in third estate, a common man,
I pray I'll live to greet that little one.

A WOMAN'S TOUCH

("Touch" panel from the Lady and Unicorn tapestries)

One hand on the pole of her father's standard, the other
grasping the unicorn's horn, she is looking at neither.

Holding to standard and horn, accepting as lover
the man her father has chosen, she's a bridge,

cannot prefer one side to the other; caged without bars,
she has no free arm to say her goodbye to her mother.

The artist seems not to perceive there may be a problem
as her duty prevents her turning away from her father,

but near her he's drawn a monkey chained to a roller;
animals scattered around her all wear collars.

She fills her role as link in a masculine order.
A lion looks on like a satisfied older brother.

THIS LION NEVER SLEEPS

Paired in heraldry with the unicorn
like sun with moon, Lion wants his rival
gone into mythic dark. Artists who've seen
no lion in life have made them equal,
reduced them to servanthood on crests.
Lion suffers indignity of a combed,
curled mane, a feathery tail, and the burden
of silence the unicorn does not seem
to mind. For now they have détente: a balance
of power, like changing seasons. A smirk
hides Lion's discontent. This will pass.
Serving lords and would-be nobles,
Lion's in training to represent a king,
the state, a nation still being formed. He'll be
strong in the sun, and when kings decline, his role's
not over. He will roar for Goldwyn and Mayer.

TRAPPED

("Sight" panel from the Lady and Unicorn tapestries)

The unicorn sees his features in the glass
held by a maiden well-born and refined.
He's at the mercy of a gentle lass
for his reflection makes the creature blind.

Wild animal, pursued by humankind,
how has this quiet moment come to pass?
Caught, not by the strong but by the kind,
the unicorn sees his features in the glass.

In native habitat he's stern as brass
and cunning as a stag; now he's reclined
forepaws in her lap, haunches on the grass,
held by a maiden well-born and refined.

Untouchable by spear and sword combined,
unfazed by bark and bite of hounds en masse,
the soft touch of her fingertip can bind:
he's at the mercy of a gentle lass.

He has turned patient, humble as an ass,
her docile servant, freedom left behind,
captured by virtue he cannot surpass,
for self-reflection makes the creature blind,
the unicorn.

SEEN AND UNSEEN

Catching eyes, mirrors were said to catch the soul,
like Narcissus' pool. Viewers drawn in,
drawn out of past perception, were drawn apart.

Triple mirrors line a dressing room,
reflections reflected, self centered,
face and flaws, transient moods, bad hair days,

skin's subtle variations, aggregate details
taken as the I, separate from any Us,
connections beyond the mirror's eye.

In the mirror, no entrapping web,
the unicorn sees a one-horned goat,
is stupefied. Where is his power, his art?

If Adam and Eve had had good mirrors
they would have needed no apple
to show them they were naked, separate.

PUZZLES

("Mon Seul Desir" panel from the Lady and Unicorn
tapestries)

She lays her necklace in a jewel chest.
Lion and unicorn lift up the curtain.
Is she about to enter for a rest?
Perhaps it's evening, even that's uncertain.

Lion and unicorn lift up the curtain.
The halo-colored lining shines in sun.
Perhaps it's evening, even that's uncertain.
Does the empty tent await someone?

The halo-colored lining shines in sun.
A curious observer may inquire
Does the empty tent await someone?
For whom does it declare "my one desire"?

A curious observer may inquire
if her beloved staked this battle tent
for her whom he declares his one desire.
A dog, for loyalty, looks on intent.

If her beloved staked this battle tent,
the pup could be his representative,
implying loyalty, he looks intent.
It's all interpretation, tentative.

The pup could be his representative.
No clue what happens when the curtains close.
It's all interpretation, tentative.
There is so little that the viewer knows.

No clue what happens when the curtains close.
Is she about to enter for a rest?
This is the little that the viewer knows:
she lays her necklace in a jewel chest.

SEEING, AGAIN

Standing
in garb of rose
grey and vermilion,
she's poised,
not posing.

Is it the one
wild strand of her hair
that persuades me
her half-smile
is genuine?

The gentle
unicorn and petite
but regal lion,
are they pets
or imprisoners?

By the gold on blue
brocade of her tent
the artist draws me
to believe she's
favored, chosen.

ELDEST TO ELDEST

> (Claude LeViste, daughter of Jean who
> ordered the Lady and Unicorn tapestries)

I know so little of you, Claude, eldest
daughter of a strong father, as I am,
a few dates, two husbands' names.
Were you blonde? Did you have a dog?
Is your face on one of these tapestries?
Feeling the blanks as if you were
my own ancestor, could I find more
by searching dusty archives?

The eldest child brings untrod territory
to the parents. Your mother bore
more daughters, no son
to displace you. Your father
swallowed this loss. My father's
losses were of different kind,
the unsold writing, books unfinished.
Both worked the cards dealt them.

Desire to please them
worked, I believe, in both of us,
as we each studied books on being
ladylike, though mine addressed
the ugliness of chewing gum,
the value of a tidy room,
yours put emphasis on pleasing God
and kind attention to the lesser folk.

You inherited the tapestries; I
a box of books. Were you a reader?
I picture you standing at a ravine
we might have called across,
but you've left only air,
a name in a catalogue, no child
to receive the weavings
or hold you in memory.

CLAUDE LEVISTE'S INHERITANCE

Father, Chateau d'Arcy,
your three crescents carved in its stone,
whispers your name. Once
I believed in unicorns, believed
I could mimic the perfect poise
of these elegant ladies, please you
standing beside my noble husband.
You wished for sons. At your end
did you suspect I'd bear neither
sons nor daughters to inherit these
fine weavings? They glare at me,
every panel decked with your banners,
women as draped statues.
Flesh, I walk cold halls
in a house in need of repair
while the whole chateau
ceaselessly whispers your name.

III. Tapestries

TAPESTRIES

Unlocking the past is
No simple matter when it's wrapped
In thick carpets of color that
Combine the daily and the dreamed.
Of the joys and sorrows of the
Renaissance there is in fact
Nothing left but threads.

HISTORIANS

When the world was half a thousand years
younger all events had much sharper
outlines than now.
                Johan Huizinga, *The Autumn of the*
                Middle Ages (1923)

The unicorn's realm a dream solidified,
we cannot leap five hundred years
to dance with the lords and ladies
of the country in which he thrived.

Admiring that age of vigor
Lucien Febvre called us hothouse
flowers. Have warm houses cooled
our eagerness for actions of valor?

The past is a mirror too distant
to give us clear sight of ourselves.
Lucien and I and Johan Huizinga
wander along cold, unswept alleys,
wanting to enter the splendid events
we are born too late to attend.

THREADS

("The Unicorn Defends Himself" from the Met
Unicorn Tapestries)

> A tapestry hound
> with his thread teeth drawing crimson from
> the throat of the unicorn
> W. C. Williams, *Paterson*

We say, "I see what you're saying,"
mixing sound and sight.
The tapestry speaks
in bright color, shape:
gold sleeves, orange
boots, brown birds,
the unicorn's white
repeated in dogs, shoes,
cuffs, each item
a separate note.

The whole, made
of silent threads, sings
a tale of contradictions.
Gabriel's horn
declares the defense
is dance, the prey
can't be captured.
Men hold back,
hounds are not so wise.
Red blood echoes
the red of tunics.

Too busy circling
back on itself to call
for attention, the tapestry
allows us to read its music,
while the world that shaped it
hides behind its tight weave.

DAMAGES

Inferior dyes on later patches
like early Kodachrome have yellowed.
Repairers sorted through scraps and batches
of flora from other weavings, followed
the pattern, hoping near matches
would be pleasing enough in the tallow
light, the owners accepting the cost
as fit for the pieces they loved the most.

Restorers today consider it dreadful,
that patching, have worked to learn
original methods, being careful
with truer threads and colors. They'll earn
degrees to become successful,
their goal not mending but a return,
although it comes at tremendous cost,
to bring us closer to what has been lost.

SIGN AND SUBSTANCE

On tapestries rabbits speak fecundity
of earth and all its creatures.

The one who ate my mother's lettuce
every spring was a dark cousin
of the rabbits caged at the county
fair, unicorn-white.

"Say 'Rabbit'" our father taught us,
"on the first of the month
before breakfast. It brings good luck."
Would it bring the prince an heir?

Don't give bunnies at Easter. Rabbits
are meant to be prey or served
on a plate. My brother has a good recipe;
I can't find the meat at my grocery.

NATURAL HISTORY

> [O]rdinary sheep are converted into a one-
> horned variety.
>> Letter from R. Lydeker to Col.
>> MannersSmith (1911) in Chris Lavers,
>> *The Natural History of Unicorns* (2009)

In high mountains to the east
shepherds meld the soft horn buds
of a newborn, healthy kid, chosen
to be the prince who leads the herd.

His cousin, the bearded unicorn,
slides into the sea of old stories
when narwhal tusks are no longer
sold as healing unicorn horns.

Sea change and oil drilling
now put the narwhal at risk,
his one long tooth not prized
like elephant tusk or rhino horn,

while the unicorn is reborn
as a horned horse, one more
endangered species
known only in captivity.

PERCEPTIONS

> In many respects life still wore
> the color of fairy tales.
>> Johan Huizinga, *The Autumn of the
>> Middle Ages* (1923)

The science-trained eye names
as magic what formerly
was simply "the way things are."

My folk wisdom is all
third hand—learned
from books, not Grandmother's mouth.

I read that every flower
has power
for good or ill. Violets

may speak love or death;
to me
they only say spring.

Summoning of spirits, prayers
to the saints;
which act caused which effect?

Those dots were connected
differently before
Newton's apple replaced Eve's.

DRAWN

Dark woods' attraction:
term it Jungian, hide it
in scholarly papers, it won't
subside. When feet can't go
the distance, imagination
trails in under trees.

Spruce in Maine, turning
maples in Pennsylvania, pines
in southern New Jersey,
losing their colors at night,
hide no unicorn, no werewolf,
not even a stray snipe.

Red Riding Hood and Gretel
tell me otherwise. Snow
White's small bearded men
were fearsome at first. Do lions
and tigers and bears still haunt
your forest dreams?

On the trail by day a deer
may startle, run. I fear none
but the male of my own species.
At night I avoid the woods,
step out on mown grass,
watching for the moon.

THE UNICORN RESTS

("The Unicorn in Captivity" from the Met Unicorn
Tapestries)

> He could slip the bond
> so lightly tied—
> if he tried.
> > Anne Morrow Lindbergh,
> > *The Unicorn in Captivity* (1956)

Someone decided the saga could not
end at death, gave the one slain
rebirth in bondage.

First tree, then collar and chain,
a fence set round like ropes
in a museum.

He is untouchable again, pure
as a young man's love before
the hunt, before trees

crowd flowers and cycles
of seed and fruit bring
youth to wisdom.

The captive's eye captures us.
In need of a myth we take him,
stripped of holly and oak,

Christ and moon. Lifted, loosed
from his surroundings he becomes
whatever we choose.

ROMANCE REMEMBERED

> "Hello young lovers,
> whoever you are."
> Oscar Hammerstein, *The King and I*

It began with loose hair, tight weave,
then curiosity, an idling engine ready to roll
around new words: *madder, weld, woad.*

A lady, a hunt, a unicorn.
The elegant lady tends her parakeet,
her puppy, patiently waiting

in France, a country of castles.
A castle requires a prince, a young man
in need of a lover to win by valor.

The unicorn moves to center stage
white as moonlight reflecting
the ardor of lady and lover.

A world so alive its mysteries shift,
shimmer: when all the questions are
answered, new ones will seed, sprout.

The centuries too wide a gap to cross,
encounter ends in absence.

NOTES

These poems circle around, describe and respond to two sets of tapestries from the years around 1500 C.E., the Hunt of the Unicorn panels in the Metropolitan Museum of Art and the Lady and the Unicorn series in the Musée du Moyen Age in Paris.

As noted in the opening poem, I began with a souvenir bookmark from Paris which presented a woman with fly-away hair. (See the back cover.) I was fascinated by the way tight weaving could portray a loose strand of hair. Only after I began exploring did the unicorns take over.

And take over they did. The unicorns in these panels are not the friendly horsey modern kind. They are goats with beards and powerful hooves, full of mystery and danger. They have multiple meanings, as do the tapestries as a whole.

The two sets of tapestries have many significant differences. The unicorn has a different role and meaning in each. The coloring, design and story are almost opposites. The unknowns of their histories are also different. And yet, rarely is one discussed without some reference to the other. Hidden behind them both is a world vastly different from ours, which is part of their fascination.

MAJOR SOURCES

Febvre, Lucien. *Life in Renaissance France*, [1921, 1925] Trans. Marian Rothstein, Harvard University Press, 1977.

Freeman, Margaret B. *The Unicorn Tapestries.* Metropolitan Museum of Art, New York, 1976.

Huizinga, Johan. *The Autumn of the Middle Ages.* [1923] Trans. Rodney J. Payton and Ulrich Mammetzch. University of Chicago Press, 1976.

Lavers, Chris. *The Natural History of Unicorns.* HarperCollins, 2009.

Williamson, John. *The Oak King, the Holly King and the Unicorn: The Myths and Symbolism of the Unicorn Tapestries.* Harper & Row, 1986.

ACKNOWLEDGEMENTS

I am grateful to Susan Bagby for giving me the bookmark and supporting my moving where it led me, and to Sandra Kohler for generous critiques of poems in progress. Others who gave helpful critique and support throughout my project include the Arroyo poets, (Richard Greenfield, Nancy Hastings, Susan Gomez, Lucille Tully, John Monagle, Claudette Franzoy, and Karen Kelly) and the Thursday Poetry Group, especially Joseph Somoza, Dick Thomas, Peter Goodman and Frank Varela.

Thanks also to Nick Courtright and Alexis Kale of Atmosphere Press for helping to make this book happen.

"Tapestries," "Threads," "Pulled In" "Historians," and "Romance Remembered" have been accepted by Sand Canyon Review for their issue on "Anemoia."

ABOUT ATMOSPHERE PRESS

Atmosphere Press is an independent, full-service publisher for excellent books in all genres and for all audiences. Learn more about what we do at atmospherepress.com.

We encourage you to check out some of Atmosphere's latest releases, which are available at Amazon.com and via order from your local bookstore:

The Unordering of Days, poetry by Jessica Palmer
It's Not About You, poetry by Daniel Casey
A Dream of Wide Water, poetry by Sharon Whitehill
Radical Dances of the Ferocious Kind, poetry by Tina Tru
The Woods Hold Us, poetry by Makani Speier-Brito
My Cemetery Friends: A Garden of Encounters at Mount Saint Mary in Queens, New York, nonfiction and poetry by Vincent J. Tomeo
Report from the Sea of Moisture, poetry by Stuart Jay Silverman
The Enemy of Everything, poetry by Michael Jones
The Stargazers, poetry by James McKee
The Pretend Life, poetry by Michelle Brooks
Minnesota and Other Poems, poetry by Daniel N. Nelson

ABOUT THE AUTHOR

Ellen Roberts Young has published poems in a wide range of print and online journals including *Dash, Sand Canyon Review, 3Elements, Common Ground Review, Pochino, Pinyon, Red Coyote* and *the Kerf.* Her chapbooks, *Accidents* and *The Map of Longing*, were published by Finishing Line Press.

Young discovered her love of research in graduate school and it was research into ancestors which led her to William Paley's *Natural Theology*, printed in 1805, which became the focus of her first full length collection, *Made and Remade* (WordTech, 2014). Paley's writing is elegant, while his theology and science offer opportunities to ponder change over time.

The gift of a bookmark from Paris drew Young to a similarly deep dive into research, this time about the world and art of France in 1500 C.E., leading to the poems in this collection.

She is a member of an active writing community in Las Cruces, New Mexico, where she is one of the poetry editors for *Sin Fronteras/Writers Without Borders Journal.*